Caribbean Social Studies 2

Workbook

T0327801

Jain Cook

Collins

William Collins' dream of knowledge for all began with the publication of his first book in 1819.

A self-educated mill worker, he not only enriched millions of lives, but also founded a flourishing publishing house. Today, staying true to this spirit, Collins books are packed with inspiration, innovation and practical expertise. They place you at the centre of a world of possibility and give you exactly what you need to explore it.

Collins. Freedom to teach.

Published by Collins
An imprint of HarperCollins*Publishers*
The News Building
1 London Bridge Street
London
SE1 9GF

Browse the complete Collins Caribbean catalogue at
www.collins.co.uk/caribbeanschools

10 9 8 7 6 5 4 3 2 1

ISBN 978-0-00-825650-0

British Library Cataloguing in Publication Data
A catalogue record for this publication is available from the British Library.

Author: Jain Cook
Publisher: Dr Elaine Higgleton
Commissioning editor: Bruce Nicholson
In-house senior editor: Julianna Dunn
Project manager: Claire Parkyns & Alissa McWhinnie, QBS Learning
Copyeditor: Tania Pattison & Tanya Solomons
Proofreader: Helen Bleck
Cover designer: Gordon MacGilp
Series Designer: Kevin Robbins
Cover photo: Przemyslaw Skibinski/Shutterstock
Typesetter: QBS Learning
Production controller: Tina Paul
Printed and bound by: Grafica Veneta SpA in Italy

MIX
Paper from
responsible sources
FSC™ C007454

This book is produced from independently certified FSC™ paper to ensure responsible forest management.

For more information visit: www.harpercollins.co.uk/green

Contents

1 Complete the crossword. All the words relate to 1.1 and 1.2 in the Student's Book.

Across

2. The quality of always behaving according to the moral principles that you believe in, so that people trust and respect you

5. A job or series of related jobs, especially a profession that you spend a lot of your working life in

10. Working in a job to gain experience (2-3-3, 8)

12. The quality of being dependable

13. A person or organisation who hires someone to do a particular job

14. A worker who has advanced qualifications, knowledge and work experience

15. Someone who is a senior experienced member of staff

Down

1. The moral principles people live by (7, 7)

3. The payment of a prearranged amount at regular intervals

4. Rules and standards of conduct that are acceptable in the workplace (4, 6)

6. A person who works for a company

7. A truthful way of behaving, speaking or thinking

8. Similar job types, grouped or categorised

9. Payment to a worker for work done in a particular time period

11. People with specialised training whose job involves using special equipment or machines

2 Read 1.2 and 1.3 in the Student's Book. Write the words in the box in the correct places in the diagram. All the words relate to major groups 1–5.

sales and services workers   professionals   clerical support workers managers   technicians and associate professionals

Major group 1

_____

_____

_____

Major group 2

_____

_____

_____

Major group 3

_____

_____

_____

Major group 4

_____

_____

_____

Major group 5

_____

_____

_____

3 Add the words below to the correct major group in Exercise 2.

bookkeeper   architect   managing director   firefighter   hairdresser dental assistant   payroll clerk   service station attendant sales and marketing   midwife   lawyer   air traffic controller hotel receptionist   construction supervisor   senior government official

4 Read 1.3 and 1.4 in the Student's Book. Write the number of each major group 6–9 that the following occupations belong to.

Major group

a) Stonemasons _____

b) Textile machine operators _____

c) Forestry workers _____

d) Fast-food workers _____

e) Train drivers _____

f) Market gardeners _____

g) Kitchen helpers _____

h) Aircraft mechanics _____

i) Subsistence farmers _____

j) Welders _____

k) Rubbish collectors _____

l) Assembly line workers _____

5 Write the name of each major group 6–9 on the lines below. Then add the occupations from Exercise 4 to the correct major group.

a) Major group 6: _____

_____

b) Major group 7: _____

_____

c) Major group 8: _____

_____

d) Major group 9: _____

_____

6 Unscramble each word and then match them with the correct definition on the next page. All the words are key vocabulary words from 1.3–1.5 in the Student's Book.

a) t e m p o r e y m u n n l e d

_____

b) y e l t e r m e a n s t o c i c a p o u n

_____

c) t r y e r i a t s k r o w e r

_____

d) n a b i r n i d a r

_____

e) v e r s e c i t r y s u n d i

_____

f) y m n e m l t o e n u p

_____

g) r y a t i e r t t r e c o s

_____

h) e l f s - d e m p y o l e

_____

i) s e l s a u s i n t r d y

_____

j) m o l m e t p e n y

_____

i) People who provide goods or services and work for themselves   _____

ii) The process of selling goods or services for money   _____

iii) Jobs where people perform simple operations using basic equipment and some physical effort   _____

iv) A situation when jobs that are available do not match the levels of training and expertise of the human resources   _____

v) Involving services rather than physical goods   _____

vi) The people who work in the sales and service industry   _____

vii) Work that you are paid regularly to do for a person or company   _____

viii) An industry that provides services instead of producing goods – for example, banks, hospitals and hotels   _____

ix) Without a job   _____

x) A situation in which a country's most intelligent people, especially scientists, go to another country in order to make more money or to improve their living or working conditions   _____

7 **Write 250 words about what you would like to do in your future career. If you are uncertain which career you would like to follow, write about your dream job.**

Think about:

- What attracts you to this job?

- How did you get interested in this type of work? Did someone inspire you? How?

- Do you have a natural talent or ability for this career?

- Have you prepared yourself in any way for this type of work (e.g. researched online, spoken to someone who already does this job)?

- What do you hope to accomplish in this career?

- Will it give you job satisfaction? How?

8 Complete the words using the clues given. All the words are key vocabulary words from 1.6 and 1.7 in the Student's Book.

a) The people and organisations involved in producing goods

_ _ _ _ u _ _ _ _

b) A situation when an employer offers short-term employment

_ _ _ _ o _ _ r _   _ _ r _ _ _ _

c) Providing services rather than selling or making products

_ e _ _ _ _ r _   _ _ _ _ s _ _ _

d) A worker who has no formal training, education or skill

_ _ _ _ i _ _ e _

e) A service that is sold to many customers at the same time

_ _ _ i _ _ _ t   _ _ r _ _ _ e _

f) Involving the extraction of raw materials and natural resources

_ r _ _ _ r _   _ _ d _ _ _ _ _

g) Part of the population that is available and able to work

_ _ _ o _ _ _   _ _ r _ _

h) Businesses that provide knowledge or skilled workers

_ _ a _ _ _ n _ _ _ _   _ _ _ u _ _ _ y

i) People who work on a full-time basis

_ _ _ m _ _ _ _ _   _ o _ _ _ _ _

j) Selling something straight to the customer for their individual benefit

_ _ _ e _ _   _ _ _ _ _ _ _ e _

k) A legal written document offering to pay someone to complete a particular set of tasks

_ _ n _ _ _ _ _

l) Turning raw material into finished goods

_ _ _ _ n _ _ _ _   _ _ _ _ _ _ _ y

9 Read 1.9 in the Student's Book and complete the qualities needed for money using the words in the box.

divisible	transactions	equal	durable	
reproducing	acceptable	difficult	uniform	portable

a) It must be _____ in order for it to be easily carried around.

b) It must be _____ to copy, to prevent people from

_____ it illegally.

c) It must be _____, with all bills and coins of _____ value looking the same.

d) It must be _____ to all parties.

e) It must be _____ and not deteriorate.

f) It must be in different sizes or _____ to enable small

_____.

10 Read 1.9 in the Student's Book and match the functions of money using the expressions in the box.

medium of exchange	measure of value
store of value	standard for deferred payment

a) It allows payments in the future to repay credit given.

_____

b) It enables transactions.

_____

c) It rates the value of goods to each other.

_____

d) It can hold its value over time.

_____

11 Read 1.8–1.11 in the Student's Book. Then use the words in the box below to complete the blank in each sentence.

money	savings	transaction need	revenue
per capita	needs	growth pole	want
	precautionary need	speculative need	

a) This area has been identified by the government as a _____ and they plan to invest heavily here.

b) Owning this house and land is known as a _____. They can always be sold to raise money.

c) Cheques, debit cards, gold or cash are all various forms of _____.

d) Over the past five years, there has been a rise in _____ income, so everyone is better off today.

e) Since the hurricane, many citizens have a _____ for money to repair or rebuild their property.

f) You may _____ a new pair of trainers to be like your friends, but we just can't afford them.

g) I don't want to touch any of my _____, because if I start, I'll spend it all.

h) Buying everyday things like a newspaper or a bottle of water is considered to

be a _____.

i) The government plans to use the _____ from petroleum sales to diversify into other products.

j) Clean drinking water, food and shelter are the basic _____ of everyone on the planet.

12 Circle the phrase in each group that does not belong with the rest. These phrases relate either to savings or budget. Say why the phrase you circled does not belong in the group. Then, on the lines provided, write a sentence for each of the phrases you circled.

a) i) eat at home **ii)** carpooling

iii) rearing livestock **iv)** unexpected illness

Why the phrase does not belong to the group: _____ _____

_____

_____

b) i) impulse buying **ii)** retirement income

iii) special milestones **iv)** annual holidays

Why the phrase does not belong to the group: _____ _____

_____

_____

c) i) avoid the stress of debt **ii)** financial independence

iii) private moneylenders **iv)** financial stability

Why the phrase does not belong to the group: _____ _____

_____

_____

d) i) other earnings **ii)** prevents overspending

iii) a financial plan **iv)** achieving future goals

Why the phrase does not belong to the group: _____ _____

_____

_____

13 Find the words listed below in the word search puzzle. These are all key vocabulary words from 1.9–1.13 in the Student's Book. The words can be horizontal, diagonal or vertical and may be spelled back-to-front.

A	B	U	D	G	E	T	C	A	N	C	T	O	N	T	G	E	Y
R	I	B	U	T	E	T	O	F	I	S	N	A	N	N	R	T	C
F	O	R	M	A	L	S	A	V	I	N	G	S	I	U	I	I	A
L	S	T	A	B	I	L	I	G	T	Y	S	N	T	L	B	D	J
H	X	J	T	D	Q	K	O	Y	X	O	N	I	I	L	X	B	F
L	G	C	E	M	L	L	X	X	D	A	D	B	H	J	R	H	S
O	K	A	F	D	O	W	G	U	L	N	A	Z	E	I	Y	Q	A
U	W	P	D	H	D	O	N	P	E	T	E	G	D	U	B	R	V
E	V	R	C	Q	A	A	S	P	S	Z	P	U	X	S	M	K	I
W	M	Y	Y	U	S	D	X	L	J	E	V	M	P	F	C	T	N
U	S	O	C	E	E	E	A	K	K	Q	P	J	D	U	F	P	G
P	J	P	C	E	S	I	R	R	G	I	L	W	K	W	Z	B	S
U	B	S	N	N	C	C	Y	Y	D	D	M	S	C	P	D	S	E
H	R	T	P	N	I	T	K	M	U	Z	L	J	D	F	C	N	V
F	F	Z	A	C	N	F	L	R	E	C	R	Q	O	S	X	A	N
S	G	N	I	V	A	S	L	A	M	R	O	F	N	I	M	T	K
Y	I	A	Z	B	B	N	E	W	R	R	T	E	D	R	E	Y	R
F	R	Q	J	E	D	R	K	Z	Z	E	V	E	I	T	K	R	F

psychologist	informal savings	expenditure
savings	needs planning	formal savings	budget
	financial stability	income

Fill in these spaces with the unused letters, starting at the top, to reveal the hidden message: __ __ __ __ __ __ __ __ __ __ __

__ .

1 **Read 2.1 and 2.2 in the Student's Book. Match the words below to their definitions.**

a) identity

i) being joined together or in agreement

b) patriotic

ii) features that belong to the culture of a society that were created in the past and have an historical importance to that society

c) heritage

iii) having variety and differences

d) cultural background

iv) the way you think about yourself, the way the world sees you and the characteristics that define you

e) unity

v) a relationship between two or more friends

f) friendship

vi) feeling of strong support and love for your country

g) ethnicity

vii) the beliefs and traditions that a group of people share

h) diverse

viii) the people related to you who lived a long time ago

i) appreciation

ix) recognising someone's positive qualities or contributions

2 **Write your own definition of friendship. Swap with a friend to see if you agree with each other about your definitions.**

Friendship _____

_____

_____

_____.

3 **Read 2.2 in the Student's Book. Unscramble the words and then match them with the correct definition below.**

a) p r o c a o t e n i o _____

b) n u h m a s c e r o s u r e _____

c) p s h i d i n f e r _____

d) g r e a t i n o t i n _____

e) m o c r i c a _____

f) t r u l a l u c y e s t i v r i d _____

g) t r a p n a c i o p i e _____

h) t r i c o t i a p _____

i) _____ feeling of strong support and love for your country

ii) _____ mix of cultural backgrounds

iii) _____ the Caribbean community

iv) _____ working together

v) _____ recognising someone's positive qualities or contributions

vi) _____ joined together or working cooperatively as a single unit

vii) _____ a relationship between two or more friends

viii) _____ employees, workers or personnel and their various skills and abilities

Was your definition of friendship the same as the one above? If not, how is it different?

4 Read 2.3 in the Student's Book and complete the statements.

a) i) _____ means showing a deep love for, and devotion to, your country. It means taking **ii)** _____ in what your country has achieved and it also means looking after your country and being **iii)** _____ and caring of other people who live there.

b) Patriotism can be shown by **i)** _____ for the environment and our national **ii)** _____, conservation and preservation of our resources and participation in **iii)** _____.

c) Caribbean countries often have one or more national emblems:

- a coat of **i)** _____, which represents the country
- the **ii)** _____ flower and **iii)** _____.

d) National emblems are a reminder of a country's

i) _____, **ii)** _____ and history, and are reminders to citizens to **iii)** _____ the heritage of the country and ongoing development.

e) The cultural heritage inherited from past generations includes:

artefacts   drawings   **i)** _____

historical monuments   **ii)** natural _____   rainforests

iii) _____ _____   stories   customs

f) Several sites of **i)** _____ and natural importance have been identified as **ii)** _____ in the Caribbean. The aim is to ensure the **iii)** _____ of these sites, as they are part of the heritage of the Caribbean. Examples include the **iv)** _____ in northern Haiti and the Belize **v)** _____.

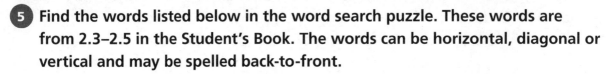
5 Find the words listed below in the word search puzzle. These words are from 2.3–2.5 in the Student's Book. The words can be horizontal, diagonal or vertical and may be spelled back-to-front.

Y	E	S	O	T	O	N	M	S	I	T	O	I	R	T	A	P
N	X	O	U	S	Q	U	E	E	M	A	W	V	P	I	A	T
O	F	P	T	I	D	U	I	T	F	D	O	A	R	T	N	O
I	O	E	S	C	O	N	S	E	R	V	A	T	I	O	N	J
T	G	R	T	P	R	I	O	U	T	I	N	G	T	U	C	O
A	D	I	A	K	U	A	T	B	E	L	H	O	E	R	A	B
V	E	F	N	N	B	L	O	C	L	L	O	T	T	I	R	Y
R	A	I	D	O	U	S	N	A	Y	A	M	O	S	S	T	I
E	L	C	I	C	E	A	R	M	U	D	R	P	U	M	E	T
S	S	E	N	E	R	A	W	A	L	A	R	U	T	L	U	C
E	X	E	G	E	A	T	T	R	O	I	F	I	T	H	G	E
R	O	I	L	A	W	A	R	E	D	M	O	I	H	L	T	O
P	R	O	F	E	S	S	I	E	U	L	L	C	A	N	U	F
S	T	O	E	X	P	L	O	I	T	A	T	I	O	N	I	C

exploitation   tolerance   cultural bonds

conservation   pride   cultural awareness

patriotism   preservation   tourism   outstanding

6 Now write the words in alphabetical order.

i) _____

ii) _____

iii) _____

iv) _____

v) _____

vi) _____

vii) _____

viii) _____

ix) _____

x) _____

7 Read 2.4 in the Student's Book and the headings in the circles. They are all to do with Carifesta. Then look at the words below. Number them according to which circle they belong to.

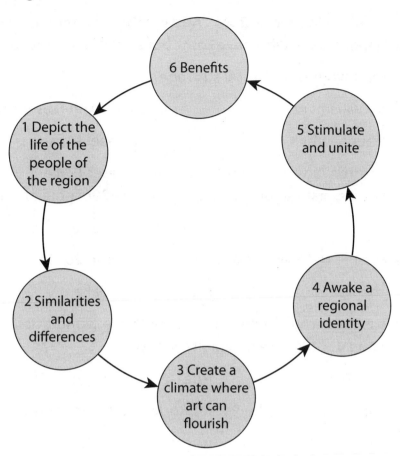

i)   Morale   _____

ii)   The people of the Caribbean and Latin America   _____

iii) Literature   _____

iv) Creativity   _____

v)   Artists are encouraged to return to their homeland _____

vi) Promotes unity and tolerance   _____

vii) Ways of expression   _____

viii) Preserves traditional knowledge   _____

ix) Promotes art and culture   _____

x)   The cultural movement throughout the region   _____

xi) Exposes people to new art forms   _____

xii) Boosts tourism   _____

8 Read 2.4–2.6 in the Student's Book. Answer the following questions about the outstanding individuals who have contributed to the Caribbean identity.

a) Who was in favour of universal suffrage?

   i) Dr Eric Williams   **ii)** Shelly-Ann Fraser-Pryce

   iii) Sir Arthur Lewis   **iv)** Michael Manley

b) Circle the correct answers about Shelly-Ann Fraser-Pryce.

   i) She was the first Caribbean woman to win 100m gold at the Olympic Games.

                        True   False

   ii) She was the IAAF World Athlete of the Year in 2014.

                        True   False

   iii) She was the second woman ever to hold the world titles at 60m, 100m, 200m and 4 × 100m relay simultaneously.

                        True   False

   iv) She helped to create the Pocket Rocket Foundation in Jamaica.

                        True   False

c) Who was the first president of the Caribbean Development Bank?

   i) Sir Arthur Lewis   **ii)** Sir Viv Richards

   iii) Michael Manley   **iv)** Dr Eric Williams

d) Who was Prime Minister of Trinidad and Tobago in 1962?

   i) Michael Manley   **ii)** Peter Minshall

   iii) Dr Eric Williams   **iv)** Sir Arthur Lewis

e) What happened to Sir Viv Richards in 1991?

---

f) In what year did Michael Manley introduce pensions for sugar workers?

   i) 1958   **ii)** 1960   **iii)** 1962   **iv)** 1967

g) What happened to Sir Arthur Lewis in 1963?

---

9 Read 2.6–2.8 in the Student's Book. Use the words in the box to complete the information about each personality. Then write the name of each person.

Nobel Prize   milk-producing   performing health and nutrition specialist   the Mighty Sparrow designing   nutritional anthropology   opening ceremonies Grenada Teachers' Awards   breakthrough   honorary degree plays   Grenada   cattle farmers   founded cattle breeder   albums   charity   artist   poetry

a) _____

Born in 1935, this singer was originally from **i)** _____. He was also known as **ii)** _____, as he always won the local calypso singing contests. He released more than 70 **iii)** _____ and dozens of singles, as well as **iv)** _____ all over the world.

b) _____

This man was a pioneering **i)** _____ who spent years observing the herds in Jamaica. He had his big **ii)** _____ in 1951 with the Jamaica Hope cattle, a specially bred **iii)** _____ cow. His continued work with cows improved the lives of **iv)** _____ in Jamaica.

c) _____

This man knew from a young age that he wanted to be a(n) **i)** _____. His talent led to him **ii)** _____ the **iii)** _____ of the 1992 and 1996 Olympic Games. In 1991, he was awarded a(n) **iv)** _____ by the University of the West Indies.

d) _____

This person was a **i)** _____. She is famous for her research into **ii)** _____ and the eating habits of African-Americans and Grenadians. She worked for a **iii)** _____ providing solar cookers to refugee camps in Africa. The **iv)** _____ programme is named after her.

e) _____

In 1992, this man, born in St Lucia, won the **i)** _____ for literature. He **ii)** _____ the Trinidad Theatre Workshop in 1959, which is still open today. He wrote more than 20 **iii)** _____ collections and 25 **iv)** _____.

10 Complete the crossword. All the words relate to this unit in the Student's Book.

Across

1. The act of looking after something so that it lasts
5. Acceptance of views, beliefs or behaviours that are different from one's own
7. Something someone can do to make a product or make it successful
9. The cultural traditions that we have inherited from past generations (8, 8)
12. How important or useful something is
13. Showing a deep love for, and devotion to, your country
15. Having variety and differences
16. Very impressive or remarkable

Down

2. A sense of who you are and that you are part of a country (8, 8)
3. Employees, workers or personnel and their various skills and abilities (5, 9)
4. Cultural ties that bring people together (8, 5)
6. Features that belong to the culture of a society that were created in the past and have an historical importance to that society
8. Joined together or working cooperatively as a single unit
10. The overuse of something
11. Feeling of strong support and love for your country
14. Being joined together or in agreement

11 Write a letter to a friend in another country telling them about your cultural heritage. Think about the traditions you follow that have been handed down from previous generations and say why you still follow them and what you like or dislike about them. Write 200–250 words.

_____

_____

_____

_____

_____

_____

_____

_____

_____

_____

_____

_____

_____

_____

_____

_____

_____

12 Write a profile of a famous Caribbean personality who you admire. They can come from any of the Caribbean countries and could be a famous sportsperson, singer, writer, etc.

Include their name, date of birth, the country they are from and a list of their achievements. Follow an example from 2.6 of the Student's Book.

Profile

- _____
- _____
- _____
- _____
- _____
- _____
- _____
- _____
- _____
- _____
- _____
- _____
- _____
- _____
- _____
- _____

1 Read 3.1 and 3.2 in the Student's Book. Then look at the map below of Guyana. Use the items in the box to label the map.

Kanuku Mountains	Kamoa Mountains	Mount Roraima
Pakaraima mountain range	Mount Ayanganna	Acarai Mountains

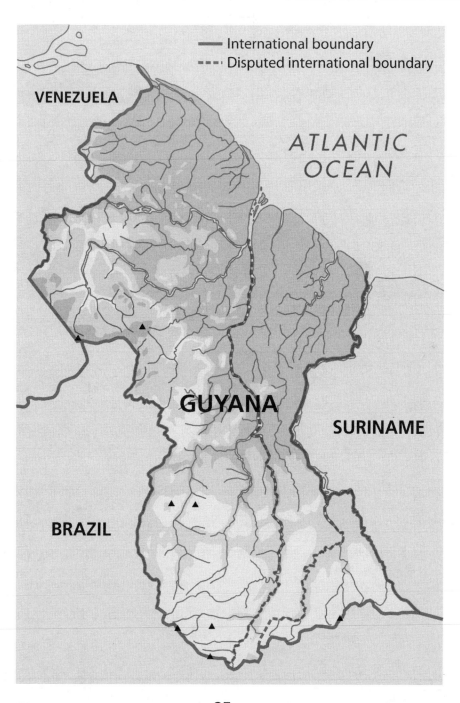

2 Complete the crossword. All the words are key vocabulary words from 3.1–3.6 in the Student's Book.

Across

3. The area of land by the sea
5. The place where a river is widest and joins the sea
9. Natural structures like very big hills that are much higher than the usual level of land around them
12. Where rainfall has filled volcanic holes (6, 4)
13. A shallow bowl-shaped limestone hole
14. A narrow area of land that continues further out into the sea than the land it is part of
15. To put notes in a piece of writing in order to explain parts of it
17. A large flat area of land
18. The process where you observe people or places (or landform features) in real locations and situations (5, 11)

Down

1. When many cracks are found within limestone rock
2. One of the very large areas into which the Earth's surface is broken up and which move against each other (8, 5)
4. A computer program used for looking for information on the internet (6, 6)
6. A simple drawing that is used to highlight specific features or landforms or to show the general landscape (5, 6)
7. Where volcanic heat warms underground water (3, 7)
8. A cone-shaped mass of material that builds up around the crater of a volcano (8, 4)
10. A landscape created from limestone
11. A narrow piece of land that sticks out into the sea
12. Say where sources were found
16. A plain of hardened lava (4, 5)
17. Something that water flows through rather than over

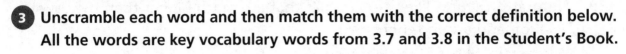

3 Unscramble each word and then match them with the correct definition below. All the words are key vocabulary words from 3.7 and 3.8 in the Student's Book.

a) clinimade spertopire   _____

b) platicor rotfes   _____

c) slaporat gnarfim   _____

d) shanavna   _____

e) brumel   _____

f) grasovmen   _____

g) especis   _____

h) bralea nimfrag   _____

i) Features of plants that can be used in vaccinations, drugs and patients' treatment

ii) Growing of crops such as sugar for money

iii) Trees, wood

iv) Trees and shrubs that grow along coastal regions in tropical areas

v) Trees that grow in a warm, wet climate all year

vi) Raising grazing livestock for money

vii) A plant or animal group whose members all have similar general features and are able to produce young plants or animals together

viii) An area of grassland

4 Read 3.9–3.11 in the Student's Book. Use the words in the box below to complete the blank in each sentence.

hazard	volcanoes	hydrological	hurricane	primary
secondary	habitats	environment	earthquake	water
fault	waves	hamlet		

a) The huge amount of rainfall that the rainforests produce each year helps sustain the _____ cycle.

b) Tropical rainforests provide _____ for hundreds of different species of wildlife.

c) A natural _____ is a natural process that can have negative effects.

d) A _____ is an intense storm with very strong winds and a lot of rainfall.

e) _____ shoot gas and ash into the air and pour lava onto the land.

f) An example of a natural hazard is an _____.

g) A _____ is a long deep crack on land or under the sea.

h) Hurricane winds cause strong _____ that beat the coast for many hours.

i) The _____ cycle is a continuous process that moves water between the atmosphere, the surface of the Earth and the spaces under the Earth's surface.

j) The human _____ refers to an area where humans live and work.

k) The smallest type of settlement is a _____.

l) _____ industries are those that involve extracting natural resources.

m) _____ industries are those that are involved with making things.

5 Read 3.13 in the Student's Book. Then label the diagrams with the names of the types of settlement they show.

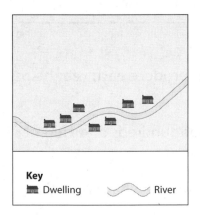

Key
🏠 Dwelling   〰️ River

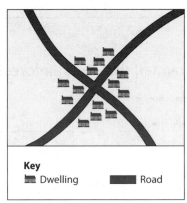

Key
🏠 Dwelling   ▬ Road

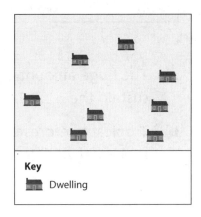

Key
🏠 Dwelling

i) _____   ii) _____   iii) _____

6 Write about the area where you live. Write 200–250 words.

Things to include:

• transport facilities and nearby roads, ports or airport

• the nearest large city

• nearby recreational facilities

• the settlement pattern

• the population of where you live

• the population density of the area

• the population distribution.

7 Match each word from 3.12 and 3.13 in the Student's Book to the correct definition.

a) Linear settlement

b) Nucleated settlement

c) Scattered settlement

d) Settlement pattern

i) Houses and buildings grouped close together

ii) Houses and buildings spread over a large area

iii) Houses and buildings built in lines

iv) Shape of the hamlet, village, town or city

8 Look at 3.14–3.16 in the Student's Book. Circle True or False for each of the statements below.

a) Approximately 7 billion people live in India and China.   True   False

b) The total population of a country is easy to understand on a choropleth map.   True   False

c) Urban areas have moderate and high population densities.   True   False

d) A choropleth map shows high density areas in lighter colours.   True   False

e) One dot on a dot map usually represents 1000 people.   True   False

f) Mountainous areas tend to have higher populations than flatter areas.   True   False

g) Savannah areas are generally less populated.   True   False

h) In Barbados and St Lucia, the coastal areas are more densely populated.   True   False

i) A major drawback with dot maps is that they take a long time to make.   True   False

j) Rural areas have more services and more people than urban areas.   True   False

9 Use the words in the box to complete the blank in each sentence.

rural areas	population	census
population density	population distribution	urban area

a) _____ is not evenly spread throughout the world, with some areas being very densely populated.

b) _____ are villages and hamlets with not many services.

c) In any capital city, the _____ is very high in each square kilometre.

d) A _____ is a way of collecting the population information of a country.

e) The word _____ refers to the total number of people living in a specific geographic area at a particular point in time.

f) I prefer to live in an _____ where it's easier to find a job and there's lots of entertainment.

10 Match the words in the box to the correct heading in each circle. The words are from 3.16–3.18 in the Student's Book.

dams	fertile farmland	not too wet or dry
road networks	hilly regions	access to services
canyons	people living in an area	not too hot or cold
moderate population	well connected to cities	wash
high birth rate	size of an area	cliffs
less rainfall	monuments	rivers
valleys	fish	bridges

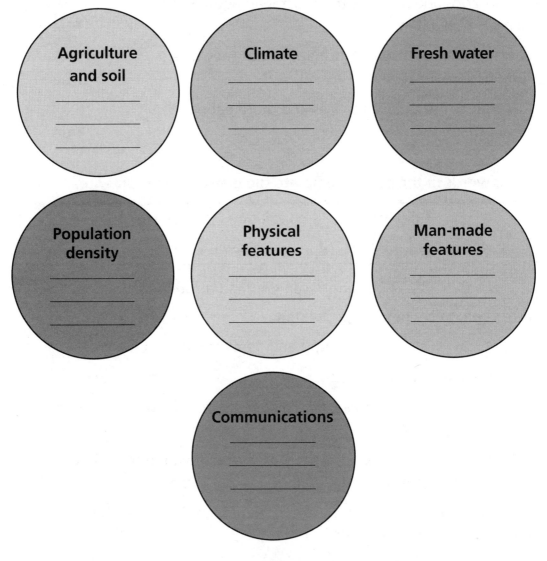

Agriculture and soil

Climate

Fresh water

Population density

Physical features

Man-made features

Communications

11 Read 3.18–3.20 in the Student's Book. Match each sentence beginning (a–h) with the correct sentence ending (i–viii).

a) Areas covered in thick, dense forest   _____

b) Fewer trees leads to more carbon dioxide,   _____

c) The land beside the sea was once covered in mangroves   _____

d) Low-lying coastlines have far more opportunities
    to farm or build   _____

e) Farming is very difficult   _____

f) The port of Bridgetown, Barbados   _____

g) When trees have been cut down,   _____

h) It is not possible to use land that floods   _____

i)   so temperatures increase.

ii)   provides a natural harbour for maritime traffic.

iii) than the higher ones.

iv)   for any form of building.

v)   are not suitable for building on, unless the forest is cleared first.

vi)   the risk of flooding increases.

vii) and completely unsuitable to build on.

viii) in mountainous and hilly areas.

12 **Complete the words using the clues given. They are from sections 3.20 and 3.21 in the Student's Book.**

a) Travel some distance to and from work

_ o _ _ _ _ e

b) Using methods that do not harm the environment, so that natural resources last a long time

_ u _ _ _ _ n _ _ _ _ i _ _

c) The management of land and water in ways that prevent it from being damaged or destroyed

_ _ _ _ e _ _ a _ _ o _

d) The main commercial area of a city

_ e _ _ _ a _   _ _ _ i _ e _ _   _ i _ _ _ i _ _

e) To take care of a place or building in order to prevent it from being harmed or destroyed

_ _ e _ _ r _ _

f) Something that means when it is used up it cannot be replaced

n _ n-r _ n _ w _ bl _   r _ so _ r _ e

g) Located just outside the city

_ u _ _ _ _ a _

h) Capable of continuing for a long time at the same level

_ _ _ t _ _ _ a _ _ e

i) Protecting something valuable so that it is not damaged or destroyed

_ _ _ s _ _ _ a _ _ _ _

j) To prevent land, water, or other natural resources from being damaged or destroyed

_ _ n _ _ r _ _

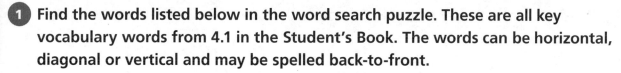

1 Find the words listed below in the word search puzzle. These are all key vocabulary words from 4.1 in the Student's Book. The words can be horizontal, diagonal or vertical and may be spelled back-to-front.

Y	E	P	W	E	Z	N	T	O	I	E	L	U	P	Y
T	I	D	R	H	D	C	G	R	O	U	P	N	H	W
I	S	O	C	I	A	L	G	R	O	U	P	I	H	W
T	L	X	L	R	M	X	I	T	O	R	X	T	E	Q
N	X	F	E	W	N	A	D	B	O	U	I	Y	I	W
E	G	T	O	B	X	Y	R	S	T	Y	P	A	K	I
D	N	O	J	R	X	J	D	Y	T	Q	X	S	P	G
I	T	R	X	S	M	O	J	B	G	A	Q	I	Z	E
S	E	C	O	N	D	A	R	Y	G	R	O	U	P	S
T	L	P	U	O	R	G	L	A	M	R	O	F	N	I
Z	Z	X	K	I	Q	F	W	G	Z	Z	S	U	G	S
J	T	O	O	T	G	P	E	U	R	P	I	W	P	N
J	K	N	Z	W	G	N	I	G	N	O	L	E	B	S
H	A	F	U	R	C	T	T	O	N	K	U	D	D	U
I	C	K	P	D	J	U	U	S	A	H	D	P	F	F

secondary groups	identity	informal group
social group	interact	belonging
formal group	unity	primary groups
	group	

2 Now write the words in alphabetical order.

a) _____   b) _____

c) _____   d) _____

e) _____   f) _____

g) _____   h) _____

i) _____   j) _____

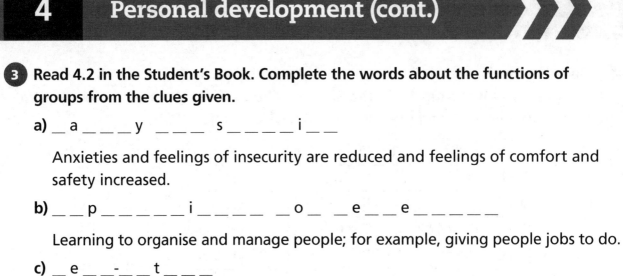
3 Read 4.2 in the Student's Book. Complete the words about the functions of groups from the clues given.

a) _ a _ _ _ y _ _ _ s _ _ _ _ i _ _

Anxieties and feelings of insecurity are reduced and feelings of comfort and safety increased.

b) _ _ p _ _ _ _ _ i _ _ _ _ _ o _ _ e _ _ e _ _ _ _ _

Learning to organise and manage people; for example, giving people jobs to do.

c) _ e _ _-_ _ t _ _ _ _

Feeling good about oneself; for example, helping other people.

d) _ _ n _ _ _ _ _ _ _ l _ _ _ i _ _ _ _ _ _ _ e _ _ i _ _

The sense of belonging and being associated with a group or a group of people.

e) _ _ _ s _ _ _ _ _ u _ _ _ _ e / _ _ _ _ i _ _ e _ e _ _ _ _

_ _ e _ _ _ i _ _ _ _ _ _ s

As a group working towards common aims; for example, raising money for a community project.

f) _ _ _ a _ _ _ _ _ _

Learning how to behave in social situations.

g) _ _ _ _ a _ _ _ _ _ _ _ i _ _ _ d _ r _ _ _ _ _ s _ _ _

Enjoying the company and friendship of other people.

h) _ _ _ o _ _ _ _ _ _ _ i _ _ _ _ _ _ _ r _ _ e _

_ k _ _ l _ _ _ n _ _ _ _ e _ _ s

Learning how to do new things.

4 Write a journal entry of about 150 words on why you joined a particular group or club. What did you hope to achieve by joining it?

_____

_____

_____

_____

_____

_____

_____

5 Read 4.2 in the Student's Book. Match the statements below to the correct heading. The statements and headings refer to the functions of groups.

a) People accept me for what I am. _____

b) I have made lots of new friends. _____

c) We have made a difference to local people's lives. _____

d) I am in charge of a group of 20 people. _____

e) I feel I really fit in with the other members of the group. _____

f) I am secure when I am with the group. _____

g) I now know how to design a website. _____

6 Read 4.3 in the Student's Book. Use the words in the box to complete each blank in the paragraphs.

Characteristics of groups

identity	membership	sanctions	hierarchy
specific	criteria	defined	interaction
clothing	rules	structure	common
qualify	authority	cooperation	symbols

a) _____ **purpose or goals of the group**

These are clearly _____ goals the group are working towards.

b) _____ set out the group's goals, are used to maintain order and behaviour, and are the _____ for membership; sometimes groups can have _____ if rules are broken.

c) _____

Depending on the group type, this is how often groups meet.

d) _____

These are the set rules for joining the group; sometimes you may have to fulfil certain criteria to _____ for membership.

e) _____ **to achieve group goals**

This is when group members work together to complete a task that is _____ to the group.

f) **Marks of _____**

Groups have these, or _____, which may be seen in the members' _____, which helps to identify the group within a wider society and encourage a sense of belonging and identity for members.

g) _____

Depending on the type, groups can have a clear structure and _____ with clear lines of _____, or there may be no clear structure in place. According to what type of structure there is in the group, its members' roles and responsibilities will be defined.

7 Read 4.3 in the Student's Book. Complete the reasons why the following groups use a logo or symbol.

a) A trade union uses a logo with

_____.

b) A Scout or Girl Guide group uses a logo as

_____.

c) A church group may use a symbol

_____.

d) A youth club may have a logo to

_____.

e) A political party may use a symbol

_____.

8 Read 4.3–4.5 in the Student's Book. Write the words in the box below in the correct place in the circles.

personal	more than three	impersonal	dyad
contribute	face-to-face	larger	formal
thousands of members	intimate	triad	loyalty

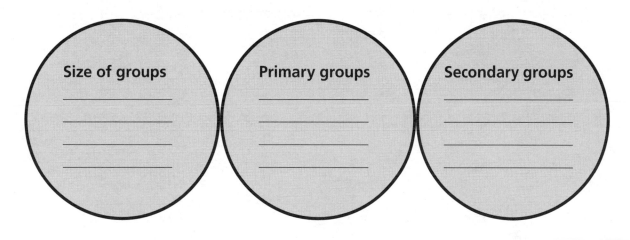

Size of groups
_____
_____
_____

Primary groups
_____
_____
_____

Secondary groups
_____
_____
_____

9 Complete the crossword. All the words relate to this unit in the Student's Book.

Across

2. System in which people are ranked according to their status or power

3. Being joined together or in agreement

5. The purpose of a particular thing or person

7. Formally assign someone to a job, role or position

9. To feel accepted or part of a group

10. Group of three

13. The way something is made, built or organised

14. A group that has written rules, a clear division of work and power, and procedures for replacing members (6, 5)

15. Small groups in which people frequently interact (often daily), know each other very well, and can depend on each other – for example, a family (7, 6)

16. The way you think about yourself and the way the world sees you

17. A sign or image that is used to represent something

18. Group of two

Down

1. Large groups which are not close or intimate – for example, a sports club (9, 6)

4. A group that does not have written rules or objectives or a strict hierarchical structure (8, 5)

6. Vote to a position in an election

8. To communicate with other members of a group

11. The power or right to give orders and directions to others, to make decisions and to enforce those decisions

12. Two or more people who do things together to achieve their common goals

13. A form of punishment, used to make sure that group members follow the group rules

10 **Read 4.4 in the Student's Book. Then answer these questions about formal and informal groups.**

a) Name the six characteristics of formal groups.

_____

_____

_____

b) Give three examples of formal groups.

_____

_____

c) Name the five characteristics of informal groups.

_____

_____

_____

d) Give two examples of informal groups.

i) _____   ii) _____

11 **Answer these questions about groups. Circle True or False for each of the statements below.**

a) A primary group is usually small in size, whereas a secondary group can have thousands of members. | True | False

b) A primary group has formal rules, but a secondary group has no set rules. | True | False

c) In a primary group, their main aim is to fulfil the needs of its members and provide care, support and security. | True | False

d) There is often emotional depth in the relationships between members of a secondary group. | True | False

e) Interaction in primary groups is intimate, informal and face-to-face. | True | False

f) Examples of a secondary group are family, people in the neighbourhood and friends. | True | False

12 Read 4.6–4.8 in the Student's Book. Complete the statements below using the words in the box.

goals	skills	belonging	effective
commitment	team	cooperation	identity

Group cohesion requires:

a) good communication and _____

b) the same _____ and interests

c) _____ from the members

d) a sense of _____ to the group

e) a good strong _____ for the group

f) _____ leadership

g) plenty of opportunities to use new _____

h) working together as a _____.

13 Read 4.8 in the Student's Book. Use the words in the box to complete the statements.

allocate	respectful	deal	goals	influential
motivate open	persuade	reliable	respect	communicate

A good leader should be able to:

a) _____ well with the members

b) _____ with people

c) set _____ for the group and put members' needs first

d) _____ resources to achieve the group's goals

e) _____ and _____ other members to achieve the group's goals

f) be honest, _____ and fair

g) command _____ of the members and be _____ towards them

h) be _____ and apply good ideas from members

i) be _____ on how people think and act.

43

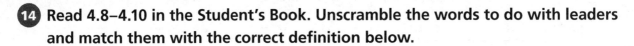

14 Read 4.8–4.10 in the Student's Book. Unscramble the words to do with leaders and match them with the correct definition below.

a) assezil-refia delare

b) lontaria-galle youtharit

c) phealsired squilatie

d) thanuriatoria aledre

e) shamricciat tryouthia

f) flestucper

g) nilotraitad ryouttiha

h) moccatride relade

i) teamide

j) bellaire

i) Power that comes from one's exceptional personality or character, or powers of persuasion

ii) Someone who discusses issues as a group and accepts the subsequent decisions

iii) A form of leadership in which people come to a position of power through a fair system of rules and laws

iv) Able to be trusted

v) A form of leadership in which people come to positions of power through customs or traditions, because it has always been that way

vi) Someone who lets the group make their own decisions in their own way, or the group members do as they please

vii) Someone who controls everything in a group or organisation rather than letting people decide for themselves

viii) To try to settle an argument between two opposing sides

ix) Personal qualities that help a person to lead others

x) Having due regard for someone or something

1 Read 5.1 in the Student's Book and answer the questions below.

a) Write down the five items that a constitution outlines.

i) _____

ii) _____

iii) _____

iv) _____

v) _____

b) What is a referendum?

_____

_____

c) What is secession?

_____

_____

d) What happens if there is anarchy in a country?

_____

_____

_____

e) What are the four main characteristics of a democracy?

i) _____

ii) _____

iii) _____

iv) _____

f) How does a direct democratic government function?

_____

_____

_____

2 Read 5.2 and 5.3 in the Student's Book. Use the words or expressions in the box to complete each sentence.

diplomatic	order	confrontational
modern states	nominee	majority rule
representative democracies	minority rights	security
direct		

a) Some actions taken by a representative democracy can also be considered as _____ democracy.

b) A _____ has the right to ask for votes to be recounted in an election.

c) A characteristic of a democracy is _____, which is when decisions are made based on most of the population's wishes.

d) There are several ways of bringing about changes through non- _____ means, including forming pressure groups against the government.

e) _____ take an individual's rights and needs into account, along with the majority rule.

f) Democratic governments are found all around the world; some of these are _____, while others are direct democracies.

g) All _____ have governments, although they are not always the same.

h) Pressure groups should try to deal with situations in a calm, _____ manner that is not aggressive or threatening.

i) The army is necessary to uphold national _____ and protect citizens.

j) In order for a country's citizens to have freedom to live without fear for their lives and property, there must be law and _____.

3 **Complete the crossword. All the words are key vocabulary words from 5.1–5.3 in the Student's Book.**

Across

3. A system of government in which a country's citizens choose their rulers by voting for them in elections

6. A vote by the eligible voters of a country on a single law or question, or to accept or reject an idea or law

8. A political system that allows citizens of legal voting age to establish rules and laws (6, 9)

10. The principles and laws by which a country is governed

11. A group of people, usually elected, who have the power and authority to manage the affairs of the country

12. When a country or group separates from a larger group

13. Careful about what you say, in order to avoid offending anyone

14. Someone who is a member of a country, and who has certain rights in the country, but who also has duties towards that country

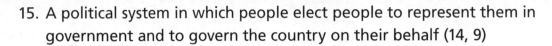

15. A political system in which people elect people to represent them in government and to govern the country on their behalf (14, 9)

Down

1. Rules or ideas that explain how something works
2. When the majority of people in a country respect and obey the laws of the society or country in which they live (3, 3, 5)
4. When the absence of a government causes a breakdown of law and order in a society
5. Where someone does not show aggression or is not hostile or threatening (3, 15)
7. Countries with contemporary systems of government (6, 6)
9. A disagreement where the parties involved see a threat to their needs, interests or concerns

4 **Read 5.4 in the Student's Book. Then, in your own words, write definitions of the following:**

a) Legislature

_____

_____

_____

b) Executive

_____

_____

_____

c) Judiciary

_____

_____

_____

_____

5 Read 5.5 in the Student's Book. Match the words below to their definitions. All the words relate to local government.

a) local government

b) constituency council

c) councillors

d) mayor

e) committees

f) Member of Parliament

g) municipals

h) constituency

i) chairperson

j) council

i) someone who represents their constituency in Parliament

ii) people who are elected to serve in local government on councils

iii) someone who leads the council

iv) an area in a country where voters elect a representative to a local or national government body

v) the part of the government that looks after government functions at a local level

vi) an administrative body in local government

vii) the council that presides over a constituency

viii) a group of people selected or elected to do a particular job

ix) associated with or belonging to a town or city that has its own local government

x) the head of a city or borough

6 Read 5.6 in the Student's Book. Which of the functions below are carried out by central government and which by local government? Write CG or LG.

a) Collecting and disposing of garbage   _____

b) Raising of revenue (through taxation)   _____

c) Building of relationships with other countries   _____

d) Providing social services, such as health and education   _____

e) Providing and maintaining community services   _____

f) Developing economic policies to help businesses grow   _____

g) Planning land development activities, such as drainage   _____

h) Maintaining law and order   _____

i) Constructing and maintaining minor roads   _____

j) Ensuring national security by providing a police force   _____

k) Overseeing infrastructure, including roads, hospitals, schools   _____

7 Read 5.7 in the Student's Book. Match the years with the events.

a) 1814

b) 1796

c) 1979

d) 1674

e) 1966

f) 1970

i) St Lucia gained its independence

ii) Guyana became a republic

iii) Guyana was a Crown Colony until this date

iv) Guyana was placed under British Crown Colony rule

v) St Lucia became a British Crown Colony

vi) St Lucia became a French Crown Colony

8 Read 5.7 and 5.8 in the Student's Book. Complete the words below using the clues given.

a) A type of government that is ruled by a king or queen

_ o _ _ _ _ _ y

b) A country with a parliament and a monarch as the head of state

_ a _ _ _ a _ _ _ _ a _ _   _ _ _ _ r _ _ _

c) A government department or the building from which it operates

_ _ _ i _ t _ _

d) A country ruled by the monarch of another country

_ r _ _ _   _ o _ _ _ _

e) Someone such as the President

_ _ a _   _ _   _ _ _ _ e

f) The political leader of a country that does not have a king or queen

_ r _ _ i _ _ _ _

g) A country that has become independent from the colonial power

_ o _ _ _ i _ _ _ i _ _ _ _   _ _ n _ _ _ _ _

h) A group of members of a government who are chosen by the leader of the government to give advice and be responsible for its policies

_ _ b _ _ _ _

i) A country that is controlled by another country

_ _ _ o _ _

j) A prime minister or leader of a country

_ _ e _ _ _ _

k) An official who is appointed to run a country

_ _ _ e _ _ o _

l) A type of government in which the leaders and government are elected by the citizens of the country

_ _ _ u _ _ _ _

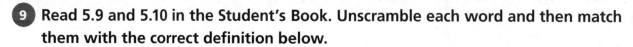

9 Read 5.9 and 5.10 in the Student's Book. Unscramble each word and then match them with the correct definition below.

a) n a t i c a d e d

b) s t r i f - s p a t - h e t - s t o p   m y s t e s

c) o r e v r o n g - n i - f e c i h

d) t r e c o l e

e) d a t i o a c e s s   e t t a s

f) t e c t o r e a l e

g) m o n s t i c u m

h) n e l t i c o e

i) t o v e

i)   A voter or person who has the right to vote in an election

ii)   People who are registered to vote in an election

iii)   A person who seeks election

iv)   A formal indication made on a ballot paper of an elector's choice of candidate in an election

v)   An official who governs a country or part of a country that is ruled by another state

vi)   A process during which voters choose candidates by voting for them

vii)   Someone who believes in a political and economic system in which individual people cannot own property or industries and in which people of all social classes are treated equally

viii) A way of counting votes in which the candidate with the most votes wins

ix)   A country connected to another country politically

10 Read 5.11 and 5.12 in the Student's Book. Answer the questions using the words in the box.

The United Nations	sustainable development	humanity
Amnesty International	justice	dignity
Rule of Law	human rights	

a) What is the principle that no one is above the law?

_____

b) What is the characteristic or quality of being kind, thoughtful and sympathetic towards others?

_____

c) Which organisation was founded in 1945, shortly after the end of World War II, to encourage international peace, co-operation and friendship?

_____

d) What is the action called when a country or region uses natural resources in a way that allows them to grow back or be replaced, and does not harm the environment?

_____

e) What is the name of the organisation that was founded in 1960 and whose work is to secure the release of people imprisoned for their beliefs, to ban the use of torture and to abolish the death penalty?

_____

f) What is the word to describe the respect that other people have for you or the sense that you have of your own importance or value?

_____

g) What words are used to describe the belief that everyone in society should have the right to liberty, equality and respect, and the freedom to express their opinions about the government?

_____

h) What do we call the administration of the law in a fair way?

_____

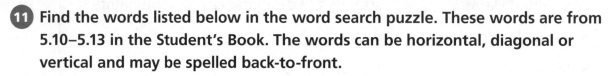
11 Find the words listed below in the word search puzzle. These words are from 5.10–5.13 in the Student's Book. The words can be horizontal, diagonal or vertical and may be spelled back-to-front.

nations	sustainable	communist	justice	dignity
human	humanity	international	development	amnesty
respect	united	rights		

L	A	N	O	I	T	A	N	R	E	T	N	I	E	T
T	S	I	N	U	M	M	O	C	W	E	S	L	H	N
N	A	T	O	J	D	U	L	D	A	L	B	W	A	E
Y	A	M	C	S	U	E	S	H	O	A	W	R	E	M
S	P	T	N	E	E	S	T	C	N	T	F	O	R	P
H	O	T	I	E	P	Y	T	I	N	G	I	D	H	O
U	E	R	S	O	S	S	A	I	N	V	W	V	S	L
M	T	P	V	O	N	T	E	C	C	U	O	T	B	E
A	N	J	Q	I	S	S	Y	R	Q	E	H	P	L	V
N	P	Y	R	U	J	K	C	O	W	G	V	G	J	E
I	E	V	S	S	O	X	C	Y	I	F	D	V	M	D
T	S	U	B	M	O	W	E	R	J	R	N	J	P	R
Y	V	H	U	M	A	N	X	Y	H	G	Z	U	K	Z

Fill in these spaces with the unused letters, starting at the top, to reveal the hidden message:

__ _____ _____ ____ _____ ___

_____.

12 Imagine that you work for Variety. Write a letter to a friend telling them what you have done for the children's charity this week. Write about 200 words.

_____

_____

_____

_____

_____

6   My community

1 Read pages 6.1 and 6.2 in the Student's Book. Circle the letter of the word or phrase that best completes each sentence.

a) People were forced to leave their homes in Africa and taken to America. This was known as _____.

   i) colonialism   ii) the transatlantic slave trade

   iii) a Crown Colony   iv) immigration

b) The slave trade was a very profitable business for hundreds of years until _____.

   i) emancipation   ii) liberty

   iii) free trade   iv) competition

c) _____ worked for ten hours a day, six days a week in very harsh conditions.

   i) Settlers   ii) Deportations

   iii) Immigrants   iv) Slaves

d) _____ is when a powerful country takes over a less powerful country.

   i) Control   ii) Raw materials

   iii) Colonialism   iv) Discontent

e) The Crown Colony system of government only represented the rich _____.

   i) economists   ii) industries

   iii) natural resources   iv) planters

f) After taking control of St Lucia in 1814, the British began to _____ the island's natural resources.

   i) exploit   ii) increase

   iii) represent   iv) appoint

g) William Wilberforce, a member of the British Parliament, took action to stop the _____ treatment of slaves.

   i) destitute   ii) inhumane

   iii) humanitarian   iv) abolish

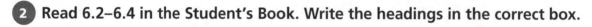

2 Read 6.2–6.4 in the Student's Book. Write the headings in the correct box.

a) Emancipation

b) Indentureship

c) Problems with indentureship

d) Farming after emancipation

e) Women in peasant farming

f) Changes in agricultural activities

i) _____

- diversification from monoculture
- people developed new skills and experience
- people able to feed and support themselves

ii) _____

- unhappy with living and working conditions
- workers mistreated and punished severely
- low wages and lack of jobs

iii) _____

- they carried and sold goods at market
- they took on sewing and washing duties
- they raised the children and kept house

iv) _____

- mass migration of ex-slaves
- squatted on land owned by the Crown
- beginning of peasant farming

v) _____

- people believed slavery an inhumane practice
- economists wanted free trade policies
- slavery was abolished

vi) _____

- slaves set up their own small farms
- immigration system set up to find workers
- workers employed for a fixed term

3 Find the words listed below in the word search puzzle. These are the key vocabulary words from 6.1–6.4 in the Student's Book. The words can be horizontal, diagonal or vertical and may be spelled back-to-front.

abolish	colonialism	emancipation	exploit
free trade	indentured	indentureship	inhumane
immigrant	immigration	migration	nationalist
peasant farming	planters	slaves	
transatlantic slave trade			

T	N	O	I	T	A	P	I	C	N	A	M	E	I	N	F	B	H	P	F	U	T	T
W	R	T	M	L	G	N	Y	T	X	I	X	N	Y	O	H	U	Y	A	Z	S	I	M
Z	T	A	M	S	E	O	K	N	G	B	D	C	N	I	G	Z	C	L	I	O	Z	K
I	Q	C	N	K	I	N	Q	R	I	E	E	F	W	T	C	Q	Q	L	L	F	J	I
I	B	L	O	S	M	L	A	P	N	I	S	V	I	A	B	A	A	P	U	W	J	K
T	W	W	O	Q	A	T	A	T	K	Z	K	I	O	R	S	N	X	V	F	O	Z	M
G	Y	Q	N	O	I	T	U	I	Y	G	C	R	L	G	O	E	M	N	J	P	T	R
T	O	P	C	O	Y	R	L	D	N	M	E	J	Q	I	J	R	O	Z	G	E	B	K
W	R	W	N	X	E	T	M	A	P	O	P	J	T	M	H	Q	M	L	O	A	X	B
S	E	G	Q	S	F	E	B	E	N	Y	L	A	D	M	S	U	H	U	B	S	X	S
O	D	A	H	R	D	D	E	Z	D	T	N	O	U	I	I	S	F	X	G	A	I	O
I	V	I	I	N	A	J	E	B	J	W	I	L	C	S	L	A	V	E	S	N	F	D
I	P	I	N	D	E	N	T	U	R	E	D	C	T	D	O	R	P	W	C	T	R	T
N	M	C	X	I	K	B	Q	P	B	M	A	M	S	Q	B	O	T	P	O	F	E	D
K	B	M	G	H	N	A	Q	N	Y	W	G	O	H	L	A	I	I	B	A	A	E	E
S	I	X	I	E	T	O	K	B	E	H	H	N	P	S	A	C	Z	Q	Q	R	T	X
L	R	B	Z	G	A	V	C	X	J	K	K	Y	U	Z	S	V	K	O	O	M	R	P
D	L	E	Y	M	R	L	T	H	W	K	U	T	X	C	L	U	E	C	O	I	A	A
K	L	N	T	P	P	A	L	U	C	L	Z	N	H	X	S	C	J	T	K	N	D	J
A	G	E	W	N	A	Y	N	I	Y	P	F	S	S	V	I	J	X	A	R	G	E	L
A	B	G	U	B	A	A	P	T	K	K	Q	Y	Z	B	X	X	B	K	F	A	Y	J
L	T	A	M	J	I	L	C	S	J	N	G	E	N	A	M	U	H	N	I	G	D	W
T	T	Q	N	V	O	E	P	G	W	B	B	O	D	Z	M	D	J	Q	V	R	J	E

4 **Read 6.6 in the Student's Book. Which of the following are primary sources and which are secondary sources? Write PS or SS next to each one.**

a) encyclopedias _____

b) bibliographies _____

c) posters _____

d) birth certificates _____

e) cemeteries _____

f) atlases _____

g) history books _____

h) furniture _____

5 **Read 6.5–6.7 in the Student's Book. Use the words or expressions in the box to complete each sentence.**

monoculture	historical site	diversification
unification	diversity	primary sources

a) There is a wide _____ of primary sources available to researchers.

b) The _____ of St Kitts, Nevis and Anguilla took place in 1967.

c) Agriculture in the Caribbean used to be based on a _____ of sugar production.

d) The _____ of crops grown meant people had an income all year and could look after themselves.

e) Nelson's Dockyard in Antigua is a fine example of an _____ visited by many tourists to the island.

f) The Barbados National Archives contains thousands of _____, such as manuscripts, wills and photographs.

6 **Imagine that you have a friend who lives in another country. They have asked you to tell them about your favourite historical site where you live. Describe the place and its history, and say why you like it so much. Write about 250 words.**

_____

_____

_____

_____

7 **Complete the statements based on your reading of 6.7 and 6.8 in the Student's Book.**

a) In your own words, write definitions of an historical site and a landmark.

_____

b) Who built Brimstone Hill Fortress in St Kitts?

_____

c) Which historical site was first built in Barbados in 1630?

_____

d) What should researchers do when looking at information from different sources?

_____

e) When does the full story of a topic come together?

_____

f) What is the oral tradition of a culture?

_____

g) Name the five ways we can show respect for historical sites.

i) _____

ii) _____

iii) _____

iv) _____

v) _____

h) What is the title of the Google Books search result for the Confederation Riots in Barbados in 1876?

_____

i) Where else can researchers go to find out further information about the Confederation Riots?

_____

8 Read 6.9–6.11 in the Student's Book. Answer the questions to complete the activity.

a) Write down the three aspects of society in Trinidad and Tobago that were affected by indentureship.

_____

b) Name one lasting effect of the formation of CARICOM in 1973.

_____

c) Identify the work female slaves did in the fields before emancipation.

_____

_____

d) Write down the work that female ex-slaves took up after emancipation and what they sometimes had to do to earn more money.

_____

_____

e) Identify the work that women could do after indentureship.

_____

_____

f) Name two areas that many women are denied access to today.

_____

g) Write down two examples of laws today that protect women.

_____

_____

h) Identify two other areas in Caribbean society that are mentioned in 6.10 that help women in the 21st century.

_____

_____

i) Name the activities that were banned in Grenada in 1885.

_____

j) What was the result of the activities being banned in Grenada?

_____

9 Read 6.11–6.13 in the Student's Book. Write the words in the box in the correct place in the diagram.

strong voice   cultural activities   universal adult suffrage

Manual and Mental Workers Union   ethnicities   hunger marches

insurrection   mediate   political franchise   economic activities

working classes   public services   imprisoned   low wages

colonial government   underemployment

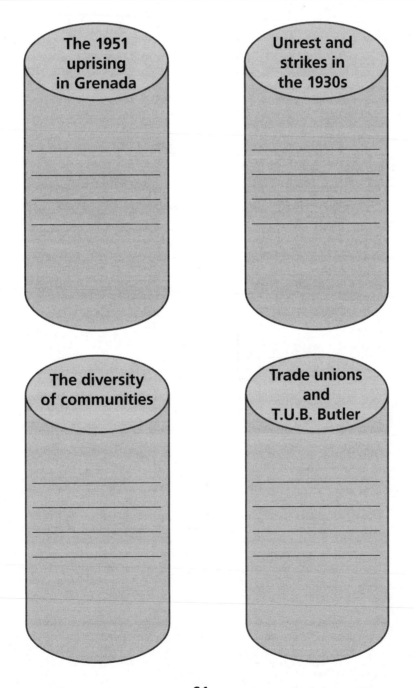

The 1951 uprising in Grenada

Unrest and strikes in the 1930s

The diversity of communities

Trade unions and T.U.B. Butler

10 Reread the key vocabulary from 6.5–6.15 in the Student's Book and complete the crossword below.

Across

6. A population moving from a rural to an urban environment (8, 9)
7. The process whereby two or more countries join together
9. Belonging to a town or city
10. Where a country uses most of its agricultural land to plant one main crop on a large scale
11. Groups in society, according to their social status; for example, upper, middle and working
12. Policies or ideas that seek to avoid or remove any distinctions between males and females (6, 8)

Down

1. Consisting of people of different cultures (13, 7)
2. An attempt by a large group of people to take control of their country by force
3. A building or feature that is easily noticed
4. Increasing and varying the types of something; for example, farming and agricultural practices
5. The right to vote in elections (9, 9)
8. Located in the countryside, away from towns or cities

11 Match the expressions with their definitions. They are all from 6.5–6.15 in the Student's Book.

gender equality   secondary source   historical site
internal migration   multicultural society

a) A document created after an event took place

b) When a person moves within the same country

c) Equal treatment, opportunities and rights for men and women

d) A society consisting of many cultures

e) A place that has special historical, cultural or social value, usually protected by law in order to preserve it

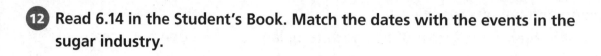

12 Read 6.14 in the Student's Book. Match the dates with the events in the sugar industry.

| 1627 | 1764 | 1870s | 1838 | 1783 | 1734 | 1795 | 1680 |

a) Antigua was producing sugar on a large scale.   _____

b) From this year, French settlers planted more cane.   _____

c) Sugar cane was first planted in Barbados.   _____

d) By this time, Barbados was a thriving
sugar-producing colony.   _____

e) After emancipation in this year, sugar cane
production dropped because of a shortage
of labour.   _____

f) By this time, St Kitts focused its agriculture
mainly on sugar cane cultivation.   _____

g) The islands of the Eastern Caribbean started to
change their economies and stopped relying
on just sugar.   _____

h) Grenada's export of sugar to Britain surpassed
that of its Windward Island neighbours.   _____

7　Our heritage

1 **Answer the questions and complete the statements based on your reading of 7.1–7.3 in the Student's Book.**

a) What do historical sites preserve?

  i) _____   ii) _____

  iii) _____   iv) _____

b) What form can historical sites take?

  i) _____   ii) _____

  iii) _____

c) When did people live who have left behind relics such as bones, cave paintings and pieces of pottery?

  _____

d) In which year was St George's Cathedral in St Vincent and the Grenadines destroyed?

  _____

e) Name the four types of places of worship mentioned.

  i) _____   ii) _____

  iii) _____   iv) _____

f) Who settled in Barbados in 1654?

  _____

g) For what purposes can a civic building be used?

  i) _____   ii) _____

  iii) _____

h) Which four government buildings are mentioned as historically important to the Caribbean?

  i) _____   ii) _____

  iii) _____   iv) _____

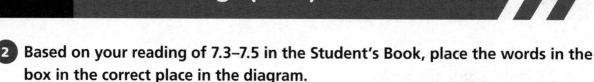
2 Based on your reading of 7.3–7.5 in the Student's Book, place the words in the box in the correct place in the diagram.

ecotourism   cultural venues   human interference   indigenous flora

genetic diversity   hiking trails   relaxation   accountability

local culture   altitude   performance arts   wetlands   managed area

entertainment   boating   Grenada carnival   ecosystem

uninhabited islands   conservation projects   natural habitats

reef-building coral   beach erosion   interpretation centre   tropical rainforest

Recreational facilities

_____

_____

_____

_____

_____

_____

Physical heritage

_____

_____

_____

_____

_____

_____

Ecological heritage

_____

_____

_____

_____

_____

_____

Sustainability

_____

_____

_____

_____

_____

3 Reread the key vocabulary in 7.1–7.4 in the Student's Book. Place the words in the box with the correct word in the circles. One word matches all three circles.

physical	ecological	genetic
natural	heritage	man-made
species		

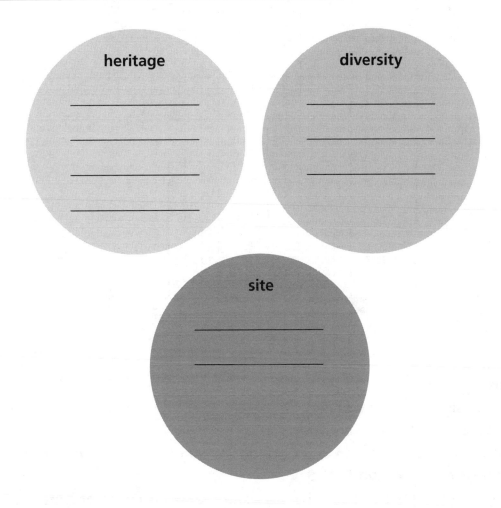

heritage

_____

_____

_____

_____

diversity

_____

_____

_____

site

_____

_____

4 Do some research on the Grand Etang Reserve, Grenada. Write about where it is, how big it is, when it was established and what it does there. Write 200–250 words.

_____

_____

_____

_____

_____

5 Complete the crossword. The words are all key vocabulary words from 7.1–7.4 in the Student's Book.

Across

2. A Muslim place of worship
6. Leisure or relaxation activities
7. A large structure that can be used for entertainment, business events or for government work (5, 8)
9. To show respect to a god by, for example, saying your prayers
10. An object surviving from an earlier time that tells us something about our history
14. Something that has been built or made by people (5, 11)
16. The great variety of life forms on earth
17. The study of the relationships between plants, animals, people and their environment
18. Native animals of a particular area (10, 5)
19. Importance or usefulness

Down

1. A holy place used by people of a particular religion, such as Hindus
3. The study of the environment and the way that plants, animals and humans live together and affect each other
4. Woodland situated between the Tropics of Cancer and Capricorn (8,10)
5. Surroundings formed by structures made by people (3-4)
8. Native plants or flowers of a particular area (10, 5)
11. A Christian place of worship
12. All the plants and animals in a particular area
13. A land environment that is regularly soaked with water
15. Features that belong to the culture of a society that were created in the past and have an historical importance to that society

6 Answer the questions and complete the statements based on your reading of 7.5 and 7.6 in the Student's Book.

a) Name the three sites in Guyana that focus on ecotourism.

i) _____   ii) _____

iii) _____

b) Name the four outdoor activities that can be done at Rewa Eco-Lodge.

i) _____   ii) _____

iii) _____   iv) _____

c) Where do guests live when they visit Surama Village and Eco-Lodge?

_____

d) What five types of animal does fauna include?

_____

e) What reasons are given for the high diversity of plant life in Dominica?

i) _____   ii) _____

iii) _____   iv) _____

v) _____

f) What is typical of flatter coral islands?

_____

g) What are plants that grow in the wetlands able to do?

_____

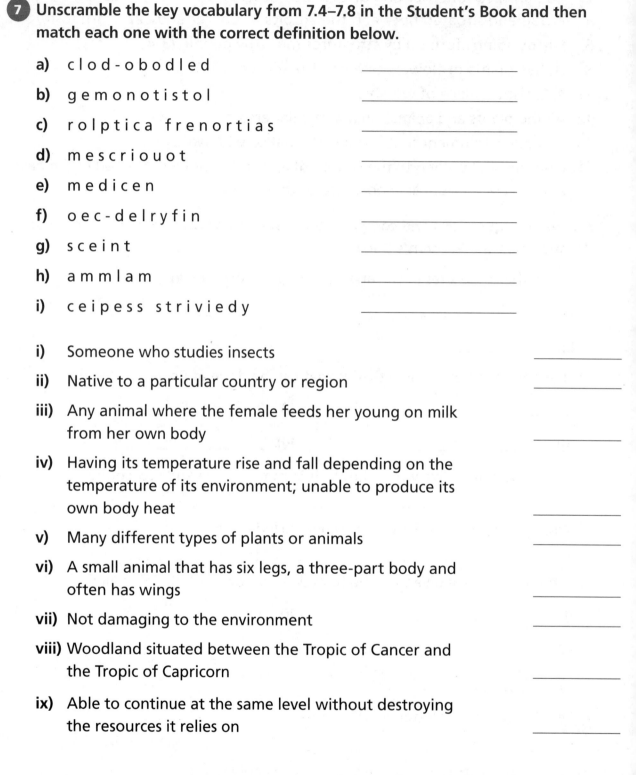

7 Unscramble the key vocabulary from 7.4–7.8 in the Student's Book and then match each one with the correct definition below.

a) c l o d - o b o d l e d   _____

b) g e m o n o t i s t o l   _____

c) r o l p t i c a   f r e n o r t i a s   _____

d) m e s c r i o u o t   _____

e) m e d i c e n   _____

f) o e c - d e l r y f i n   _____

g) s c e i n t   _____

h) a m m l a m   _____

i) c e i p e s s   s t r i v i e d y   _____

i) Someone who studies insects   _____

ii) Native to a particular country or region   _____

iii) Any animal where the female feeds her young on milk from her own body   _____

iv) Having its temperature rise and fall depending on the temperature of its environment; unable to produce its own body heat   _____

v) Many different types of plants or animals   _____

vi) A small animal that has six legs, a three-part body and often has wings   _____

vii) Not damaging to the environment   _____

viii) Woodland situated between the Tropic of Cancer and the Tropic of Capricorn   _____

ix) Able to continue at the same level without destroying the resources it relies on   _____

8 Read 7.9 and 7.10 in the Student's Book. Use the words in the box to complete the blank in each sentence.

glucose	pollution	nutrients	Equator
erosion	photosynthesis	buffer	brackish water
insolation	biodiversity	mangroves	

a) The farming industry relies on mangroves to help to ensure the balance of _____ in the water and soil because they act as filters.

b) Some wetlands have a mix of salty and fresh water called _____.

c) Photosynthesis is the process plants use to change water and carbon dioxide into food called _____.

d) The trees of the rainforest prevent soil _____ by breaking the fall of raindrops on their way to the ground.

e) _____ is when green plants and trees combine carbon dioxide and water, using energy from sunlight, to produce their own food.

f) _____ have special roots that grow away from the main tree and grow upwards out of the mud.

g) The roots of plants in the wetlands trap water from storm swells or high tides, preventing it from pushing too far inland, creating a protective _____ zone.

h) The plants in Guyana have plenty of sunlight and heat because the island is near the Equator. This is called _____.

i) Guyana contains the best examples of true rainforest in the Caribbean because it is closest to the _____, where the solar energy from the sun's rays is strongest.

j) Rainforests have an extremely high level of _____, with thousands of species of plants and insects, and hundreds of different animals all living together.

k) Trees absorb _____ from the atmosphere, such as nitrogen oxide, carbon monoxide, ozone and other chemicals.

9 Read 7.9–7.12 in the Student's Book and complete the words using the clues given.

a) Trees whose roots are above the ground and grow along coasts or on the banks of large rivers

_ a _ _ _ _ _ s

b) A type of volcanic rock

_ _ _ a _ t

c) A long solid mass that lies just below the surface of the sea

_ _ _ a _   _ e _ _

d) The process of wearing away the land

_ _ _ _ i _ _

e) A sugar that is produced in plants through photosynthesis

_ _ u _ o _ _

f) A barrier to prevent damage

_ _ _ _ e _

g) A place where water falls over the edge of a steep cliff

_ a _ _ _ _ a _ _

10 Now write a sentence using each of the words from Exercise 9.

a) _____

b) _____

c) _____

d) _____

e) _____

f) _____

g) _____

11 **Read 7.13 in the Student's Book. Then read the questions and circle True or False.**

a) Humans clear land in order to save endangered species.

<blockquote>

True   False

</blockquote>

b) When an entire species has disappeared, it has become extinct.

<blockquote>

True   False

</blockquote>

c) Some species are endangered because their habitat has been destroyed.

<blockquote>

True   False

</blockquote>

d) Overfishing is not a reason for some species becoming endangered.

<blockquote>

True   False

</blockquote>

e) Many species cannot repopulate themselves quickly enough to avoid becoming an endangered species.

<blockquote>

True   False

</blockquote>

f) Human behaviour is affecting the numbers of many species.

<blockquote>

True   False

</blockquote>

g) Scientists always know exactly how many of a species are left.

<blockquote>

True   False

</blockquote>

h) The population of leatherback turtles is thriving.

<blockquote>

True   False

</blockquote>

i) The Imperial Amazon parrot is one of St Vincent's endangered birds.

<blockquote>

True   False

</blockquote>

j) There are no other animals in the Caribbean that are endangered.

<blockquote>

True   False

</blockquote>

12 Correct the False sentences in Exercise 11.

- _____

  _____

- _____

  _____

- _____

  _____

- _____

  _____

- _____

  _____

13 Find the words listed below in the word search puzzle. These words are from 7.12 and 7.13 in the Student's Book. The words can be horizontal, diagonal or vertical and may be spelled back-to-front.

E	X	T	I	N	C	T	I	O	N	H	U	M
A	N	N	S	A	R	E	E	N	D	A	N	G
E	R	D	I	K	N	G	M	A	N	E	Y	P
A	N	I	A	M	A	L	S	L	R	V	W	O
H	Y	E	T	N	G	F	L	A	K	R	Y	L
B	L	C	M	E	G	Y	N	T	Z	E	P	L
T	C	N	I	T	X	E	C	W	C	S	K	U
R	T	O	C	W	D	S	R	W	F	N	O	T
Z	U	B	L	K	U	S	V	E	E	O	W	I
I	Q	U	E	B	X	S	Q	G	D	C	T	O
T	E	N	V	F	P	T	S	G	B	G	Y	N

conserve	pollution
endangered	extinct
	extinction

Fill in these spaces with the unused letters, starting at the top, to reveal the hidden message:

_ _ _ _ _ _   _ _ _   _ _ _ _ _ _ _ _ _ _ _ _ _ _   _ _ _ _ _ _ _.

1 Read 8.1 and 8.2 in the Student's Book. Complete the table about natural resources that have a negative impact on the environment. Use the words in the box.

houses	global hydrological cycle	heats
sulphur dioxide	climate change	vehicles
soil erosion	global warming	oil spills
power	dangerous gases	furniture
flooding	planes	creates pollution

Natural resource	Used for	Impact on the environment
Coal	a) _____ and heating homes	Creates h) _____ from the thick smoke; releases i) _____
Oil	fuel to power b) _____ and c) _____; also d) _____ homes	Releases j) _____ into the atmosphere; can result in k) _____
Gas	e) _____ electricity	Emissions cause l) _____ and m) _____
Wood	making f) _____ and g) _____	Affects the n) _____; threat of increased o) _____; deforestation leads to p) _____

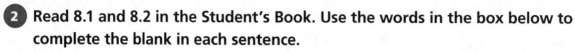

2 **Read 8.1 and 8.2 in the Student's Book. Use the words in the box below to complete the blank in each sentence.**

natural resources	extracted	mining
renewable	non-renewable	pollute
global warming	deforestation	greenhouse gases
coal	oil	carbon dioxide

a) _____ can affect the water cycle, the continuous movement of water around the world.

b) _____ are materials that form naturally in or on the Earth.

c) _____ resources can be constantly replaced and will never be used up, for example water and sunlight.

d) When fuels are burned, they release dangerous gases into the atmosphere. One of the most dangerous of these is _____.

e) _____ resources cannot be replaced. Once they have been used up, they are gone for good, for example fossil fuels such as gas.

f) The overuse and burning of fossil fuels such as coal, oil and gas, as well as destruction of rainforests, can lead to _____.

g) Natural resources have to be _____ from the Earth. _____ is a common way of extracting natural resources like coal, gold and tin.

h) Too much carbon dioxide, methane, nitrous oxide and the other _____ in the atmosphere leads to an increase in global temperature.

i) Burning coal creates thick smoke that can _____ towns and cities.

j) _____ is used as a fuel, to power vehicles and planes. It is also used to heat homes.

k) _____ is mainly used for power and heating homes.

3 Write the words in the box in the correct place in the diagram. All the words are from 8.3 in the Student's Book. These are the five strategies that CARICOM would like to introduce.

that consider marine biodiversity	will affect the environment, to reduce or avoid pollution	and clean energy options (like solar power) wherever possible	to monitor environmental changes so that countries can respond to these changes quickly

study	benefit	focus	use	improve

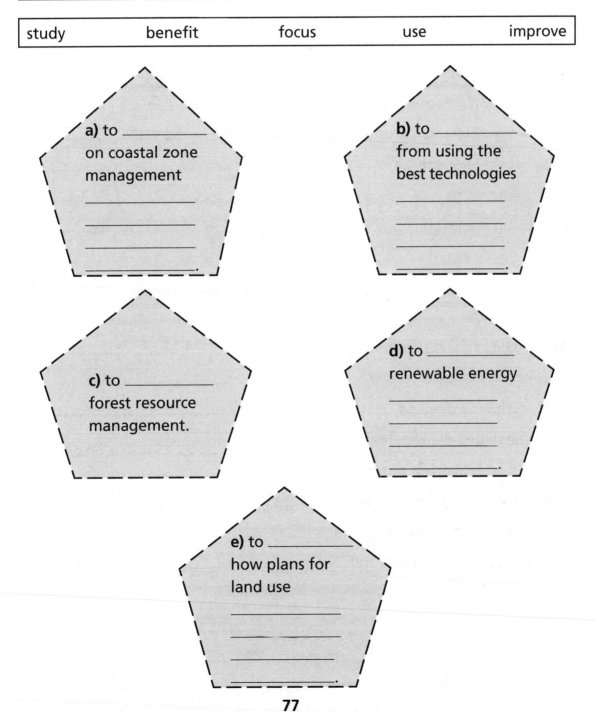

a) to _____ on coastal zone management _____ _____ _____ _____

b) to _____ from using the best technologies _____ _____ _____ _____

c) to _____ forest resource management.

d) to _____ renewable energy _____ _____ _____ _____

e) to _____ how plans for land use _____ _____ _____ _____

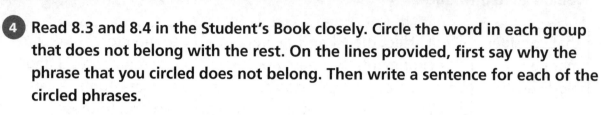

4 Read 8.3 and 8.4 in the Student's Book closely. Circle the word in each group that does not belong with the rest. On the lines provided, first say why the phrase that you circled does not belong. Then write a sentence for each of the circled phrases.

a) i) marine ecosystems _____

   ii) coral reefs _____

  iii) carbon footprint _____

  iv) commercial fishing _____

b) i) watershed degradation _____

   ii) renewable energy resources _____

  iii) geothermal energy _____

  iv) solar energy _____

c) i) rising sea levels _____

   ii) natural resources _____

  iii) coastal land _____

  iv) wetlands _____

d) i) quality of water resources _____

   ii) non-renewable energy _____

  iii) increasing demand _____

  iv) watershed degradation _____

e) i) public awareness programmes _____

   ii) environmental standards _____

  iii) reduce energy waste _____

  iv) analyse air, soil and water _____

5 Complete the crossword. The words are all key vocabulary words from 8.1–8.3 in the Student's Book.

Across

6. Things that can never be replaced (3-9, 9)
11. The continuous movement of water around the world (6, 12, 5)
12. The ability to recover quickly from a problem
13. Items that can be constantly replaced and will never be used up (9, 9)
14. The slow increase in the temperature of the Earth (6, 7)
15. Items used to make something else (3, 9)

Down

1. Carbon dioxide that forms naturally in the atmosphere (10, 3)
2. Capable of continuing for a long time at the same level
3. Items such as coal, gas or oil (6, 5)
4. Taken out
5. Stop or catch something before it can go somewhere else
7. The amount of carbon dioxide that a person, organisation or building produces, and how it affects the environment (6, 9)
8. The process whereby earth is gradually removed by wind, rain or sea (4, 7)
9. To make air, water or land too dangerous or dirty for people to use in a safe way
10. When liquid escapes from a pipeline or tanker (3, 5)

6 Look at 8.4–8.6 in the Student's Book. Circle True or False for each of the statements below.

a) An objective of The National Forestry Policy is to ensure the unsustainable use of forests.   True   False

b) The National Forestry Policy also aims to raise public awareness of the cultural value of forests.   True   False

c) The Environmental Management Authority conducts analyses of air, soil and water.   True   False

d) Internal migration is when someone moves from one country to another.   True   False

e) One push factor is living through a natural disaster. A pull factor is then moving somewhere for better living conditions.   True   False

f) A pull factor for many people when moving from an urban area to a rural area is the possibility of finding employment.   True   False

g) Pull factors encourage people to move to a new location, often for a negative reason.   True   False

h) A high population density means that there are many people living per kilometre.   True   False

i) Unemployment is when a person in the labour force is capable and willing to work, but has not yet found a job.   True   False

j) The Commonwealth Immigration Act made it hard for people from the Caribbean to migrate to the UK.   True   False

k) OECS member state citizens are allowed to migrate freely to take advantage of work opportunities.   True   False

7 Correct the False sentences in Exercise 6 in your notebook.

8 Look at the map below and the list of tourist sites in the Eastern Caribbean. Draw a line from each box listing the attractions to the correct island on the map to which they belong.

The Pitons
  (UNESCO World Heritage Site)
Marigot Bay
Reduit Beach
Diamond Botanical Gardens
  and Waterfall
Suphur Springs Park
The town of Soufrière
Anse Chastanet Marine National Park

Fort Shirley
Champagne Reef
Soufrière Scott's Head Marine Reserve
Morne Trois Pitons National Park
  (UNESCO World Heritage Site)
The Cabrits Historical and Marine Park
Dominica Botanic Gardens, Parrot
  and Small Animal Sanctuary

Brimstone Hill Fortress National Park
  (UNESCO World Heritage Site)
Frigate Bay
Mount Liamuiga
Sandy Point National Marine Park

Bridgetown and its Historic Garrison
  (UNESCO World Heritage Site)
Harrison's Cave
Bathsheba
Folkstone Marine Park and Museum
St Nicholas Abbey
Andromeda Botanical Gardens
Carlisle Bay

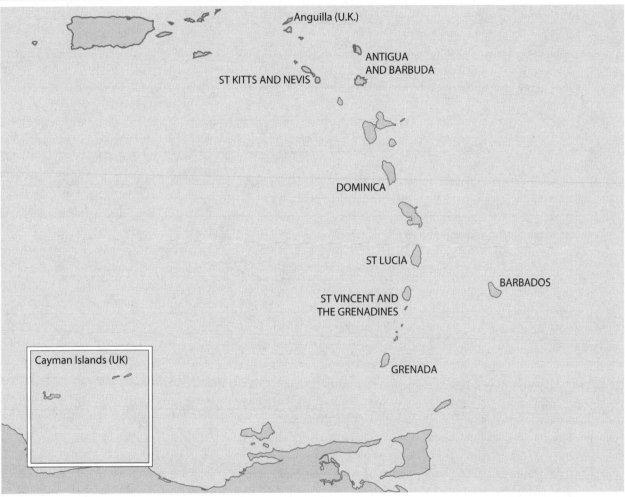

Anguilla (U.K.)

ANTIGUA
AND BARBUDA

ST KITTS AND NEVIS

DOMINICA

ST LUCIA

BARBADOS

ST VINCENT AND
THE GRENADINES

Cayman Islands (UK)

GRENADA

Wallblake House
Shoal Bay
Katouche Caves
Fountain Cavern National Park
Stoney Bay Marine Park
Sandy Ground Beach

Tobago Cays Marine Park
Fort Charlotte
Darkview Falls
Falls of Baleine
La Soufrière National Park
Layou Petroglyph Park
Bequia

Fort George
Cayman Island Turtle Farm
Stingray City
Seven Mile Beach
Booby Pond Nature Reserve

Nelson's Dockyard
  (UNESCO World Heritage Site)
Dickenson Bay
The city of St John's, Antigua
Museum of Antigua and Barbuda

Fort Frederick
Grand Etang National Park
Carriacou's Oyster Bed Mangrove
Mount Hartman Dove Sanctuary
Grand Anse Beach

9. Write a letter to your friend who lives overseas. Tell him or her about how important tourism is to where you live. Say how it benefits your country. Write 200–250 words.

_____

_____

_____

_____

_____

_____

_____

_____

_____

_____

_____

_____

_____

_____

_____

_____

_____

_____

_____

_____

_____

_____

_____

10 Write the words from the circle below under the correct heading. All the words
are from 8.7–8.9 in the Student's Book.

Climate	Flora	Fauna
_____	_____	_____
_____	_____	_____
_____	_____	_____
_____	_____	_____

social services

some rainfall   sea turtles   waterfalls

vegetation   reptiles   crime rate

plantation houses   indigenous cultures   reef fish

mangroves   telecommunications   ecosystems   colonial-era buildings

tropical   sandy beaches   warm and dry

creole languages   running water   amphibians

montane forests   mountains

seasons   lakes

Natural sites	Social and economic stability	Heritage
_____	_____	_____
_____	_____	_____
_____	_____	_____
_____	_____	_____

11 Find the words listed below in the word search puzzle. These are all key vocabulary words from 8.4–8.10 in the Student's Book. The words can be horizontal, diagonal or vertical and may be spelled back-to-front.

remittance	watershed degradation	pull factor
amenities	external migration	employed
resort	urban–rural migration	climate
brain drain	upward mobility	urbanisation
creole language	interconnectedness	push factor
multiplier effect	rural–urban migration	unemployed

N	E	E	U	N	B	P	G	F	A	K	J	C	Q	N	G	X	R	R	N
M	O	X	X	S	O	A	U	M	K	B	M	A	O	F	K	P	A	O	O
U	I	I	R	T	G	I	E	S	F	U	M	H	V	A	A	I	I	T	I
L	E	X	T	I	E	N	T	N	H	T	E	H	R	N	K	T	B	C	T
T	F	T	K	A	I	R	H	A	E	F	Z	D	U	J	A	K	W	A	A
I	A	M	A	T	D	C	N	G	S	W	A	P	Z	R	K	T	B	F	R
P	A	V	I	M	I	A	A	A	P	I	W	C	G	I	E	H	R	L	G
L	V	E	E	Q	I	Q	R	R	L	A	N	I	T	C	P	Z	A	L	I
I	S	W	C	A	U	L	O	G	R	M	M	A	N	O	X	F	I	U	M
E	T	L	C	D	H	O	C	D	E	N	I	A	B	C	R	J	N	P	L
R	R	H	R	Q	O	N	M	U	A	D	T	G	D	R	V	S	D	O	A
E	O	E	P	O	M	O	X	B	A	T	D	U	R	M	U	F	R	P	R
F	S	Z	N	P	B	B	R	Z	I	U	E	E	L	A	O	W	A	T	U
F	E	S	E	I	G	U	I	M	C	Z	E	U	H	F	T	H	I	O	R
E	R	Y	L	C	L	B	E	I	O	O	T	Y	Z	S	A	I	N	L	N
C	Z	I	T	A	D	R	B	M	O	D	A	W	M	C	R	D	O	U	A
T	T	K	R	U	N	E	M	P	L	O	Y	E	D	S	M	E	O	N	B
Y	T	U	E	G	A	U	G	N	A	L	E	L	O	E	R	C	T	Z	R
Z	R	D	E	Y	O	L	P	M	E	K	K	O	U	R	Z	B	D	A	U
I	N	T	E	R	C	O	N	N	E	C	T	E	D	N	E	S	S	I	W

12 Write the words and phrases from Exercise 12 in alphabetical order.

a) _____ b) _____

c) _____ d) _____

e) _____ f) _____

g) _____ h) _____

i) _____ j) _____

k) _____ l) _____

m) _____ n) _____

o) _____ p) _____

q) _____ r) _____

13 Complete the words using the clues given. The words are from 8.11 and 8.12 in the Student's Book.

a) A destination port

_ o _ _ - _ _ - _ a _ _

b) Damage to bodies of water through dumping of sewage or water activities

_ _ _ _ r _ o _ _ _ _ _ i _ _

c) When the quality of the soil is reduced because of extreme weather or human activities

_ _ _ _ _ e _ _ a _ _ _ _ _ _ _

d) Money paid by cruise ships to use the facilities at a port

_ e _ _ _ _ _

e) The place a cruise ship starts from

_ _ _ e _ o _ _

f) Dangerous or annoying levels of noise, caused by human activities

_ _ _ _ e _ _ l _ _ _ _ _ _

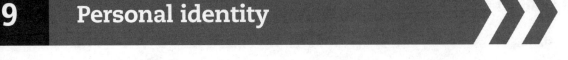

9 Personal identity

1 **Read 9.1 in the Student's Book. Match the belief systems to the correct religion.**

a) To look after the young, care for the sick and look after the elderly

b) Respecting, nurturing and caring for children

c) Living a moral life by following the Ten Commandments

d) Recognising the difference between right and wrong

e) Not harbouring prejudice or discrimination against anyone

f) Showing love, respect and kindness for all humankind

g) Working selflessly for others and living a good life

h) To uphold justice and to live a peaceful life

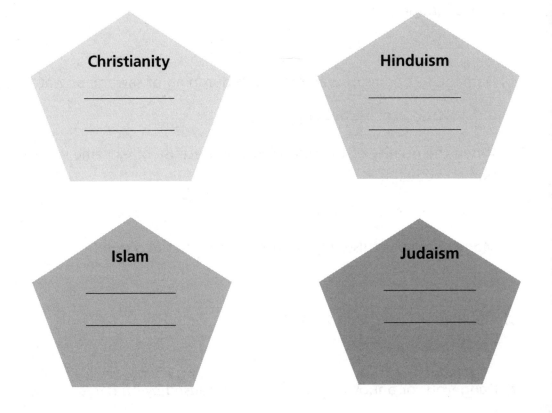

2 Read 9.2 and 9.3 in the Student's Book and then answer the questions.

a) Write the word that makes us different from each other.

_____

b) What is the word to describe the things that are the same about each other?

_____

c) _____ is the word used to say what we think is right or wrong.

d) Name what we should notice about people to understand that people are unique individuals.

i) _____

ii) _____

iii) _____

iv) _____

e) The common characteristics we share with people are:

i) _____ **ii)** _____

iii) _____ **iv)** _____

v) _____ **vi)** _____

vii) _____ **viii)** _____

f) The Caribbean has many festivals that celebrate the _____

of the different cultures that live on the islands.

g) Name the three different values that exist in our society.

i) _____

ii) _____

iii) _____

3 Complete the value words from the word cloud in 9.3 in the Student's Book with the clues given.

a) Very interested in something or excited by it

_ _ t _ _ _ i _ _ _ i _

b) Always ready to assist someone else

_ e _ _ _ u _ _ e _ _

c) Kind, helpful and sympathetic towards other people

c _ _ i _ _

d) Giving people more of your time or money than is usual or expected

_ e _ _ r _ _ _

e) Deserving of trust or confidence; dependable; reliable

_ r _ _ _ _ o _ _ h _

f) With a lot of imagination and new ideas

_ _ _ _ t _ _ e

g) Honesty and sincerity

_ _ u _ _ f _ _ n _ _ _

h) The quality of doing what someone expects them to do

_ _ l _ _ b _ _ i _ _

i) Showing that you care about other people and want to help them

_ _ n _ _ e _ _

j) Acceptance of other people's beliefs, way of life, etc., without criticism

_ o _ _ r _ _ c _

4 Write a sentence for each of the words used in Exercise 3.

a) _____

_____

b) _____

_____

c) _____

_____

d) _____

_____

e) _____

_____

f) _____

_____

g) _____

_____

h) _____

_____

i) _____

_____

j) _____

_____

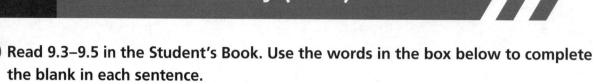

5 **Read 9.3–9.5 in the Student's Book. Use the words in the box below to complete the blank in each sentence.**

temperance	substance abuse	justice
fortitude peer pressure	virtues	morals
consequences	risky behaviour	prudence

a) Someone who has good _____ is valued as honest, respectful, kind and forgiving.

b) There are four moral _____ around which all the others are based.

c) To do one's moral duty through good actions and behaviour, one has to show

_____.

d) If someone is fair to everyone and treats them all the same way, it means

showing _____.

e) _____ means showing courage and standing up to all the hardships of life.

f) _____ is an example of showing restraint and self-control.

g) _____ is when someone your own age tries to get you to do something you do not really want to do.

h) Young people need to think about the _____ of their actions if they give in to their friends.

i) _____ is any action that can affect your current or future wellbeing.

j) Any form of _____ is very bad for our health.

6 Complete the crossword. All the words relate to this unit in the Student's Book.

Across

3. The qualities that make a person different from others

7. Having variety and differences

11. People, why they are here on Earth or their purpose
or meaning in life (5, 9)

12. People who are the same age or status as you

13. The Hindu goal of becoming one with Brahma, and release from the cycle of
reincarnation

14. What we believe is important in life

15. What is morally right or wrong

Down

1. Things that are the same in some ways

2. Actions that can negatively affect a person's current or future wellbeing (5, 9)

4. The four principles the Roman Catholic Church asks people to follow (5, 7)

5. Qualities that someone has that are thought to be morally good

6. The need and right to honour and respect

8. The customs, arts, language, history and ideas of a group

9. The only one of its kind; unlike any other

10. When someone does something because their friends are doing it, but they don't
necessarily want to do it (4, 8)

14. The principles by which people choose to live (5, 6)

7 **Read the word cloud in 9.6 in the Student's Book. Match the words about virtues to their definition.**

a) compassion

i) Thinking about the feelings and needs of other people

b) gracious

ii) Able to wait for a long time or deal with a difficult situation without becoming angry or upset

c) humble

iii) A feeling of sympathy for someone who is in a bad situation because you understand and care about them

d) patient

iv) Willing to support, work for, or be a friend to someone, even in difficult times

e) modest

v) Not proud and not thinking that you are better than other people

f) considerate

vi) Allowing someone to become part of a group or community and making them feel welcome

g) discipline

vii) Sensible, reliable and able to be trusted to do the right thing

h) loyal

viii) Showing kindness and good manners

i) responsible

ix) The ability to control one's own behaviour

j) acceptance

x) Not liking to talk about themselves, their achievements, or their abilities, even if they are successful

8 **Read 9.7 in the Student's Book. Then answer the questions about a person's role in the family.**

a) Name the people who are part of the three roles in the family and what their responsibilities are.

i) _____

ii) _____

iii) _____

_____

_____

_____

b) Write the examples of family responsibilities according to the Student's Book.

i) _____

ii) _____

iii) _____

iv) _____

v) _____

vi) _____

vii) _____

viii) _____

c) Name the four main roles that children take on within the family.

i) _____

ii) _____

iii) _____

iv) _____

9 Write a journal entry of about 250 words about your place in the family. Explain why you believe this is so, and give examples. Use the chart on page 271 in the Student's Book to help you.

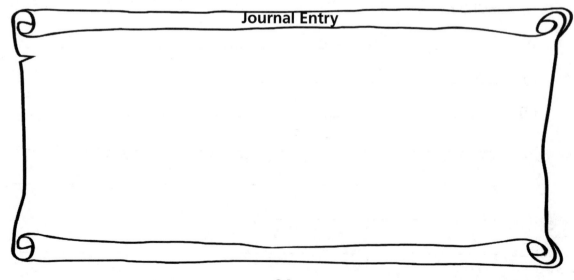

Journal Entry

10 Find the words listed below in the word search puzzle. These words are from 9.8 in the Student's Book. The words can be horizontal, diagonal or vertical and may be spelled back-to-front.

Y	S	R	C	E	L	I	G	G	I	N	O	N	N	R
T	H	P	E	O	L	N	N	P	E	S	O	U	E	S
I	U	N	I	D	M	I	U	T	E	I	R	L	S	T
R	A	N	D	R	E	M	W	R	T	O	A	U	R	S
U	E	L	V	B	I	O	U	A	T	T	E	S	B	E
C	T	T	L	E	R	T	S	N	I	U	R	O	A	L
E	L	L	M	K	O	I	U	O	I	J	R	N	E	U
S	E	O	G	D	L	P	N	A	K	T	E	E	F	J
W	L	I	J	A	H	S	Y	F	L	N	Y	N	H	O
V	V	V	I	P	H	X	M	T	M	L	L	F	P	C
J	P	C	L	I	W	P	Q	B	Y	V	Y	Q	K	Y
U	O	E	P	P	G	M	M	R	G	C	B	Z	L	L
S	M	S	R	X	R	J	N	Y	B	Y	W	D	G	J

socialisation

relationships

spiritually

nurture

security

community

wellbeing

network

Fill in these spaces with the unused letters, starting at the top, to reveal the hidden message: _ _ _ _ _ _ _ _ _ _ _ _ _ _ _

_ _ _ _ _ _ _ _ _ _ _ _ _ _ _ _ _ _ _ _ _ _ _ _ _.

11 Reread the key vocabulary in 9.5–9.8 in the Student's Book. Then unscramble each word and match them with the correct definition.

a) lyasuxel stintramdet edaisess

b) thifa yunommict

c) glebingon

d) specavenerer

e) typerbu

f) flebie mystes

g) scaltioniosai

h) squilatie

i) leor

j) tyetidni

95

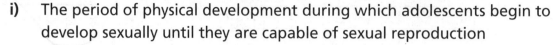
i) The period of physical development during which adolescents begin to develop sexually until they are capable of sexual reproduction

ii) How we interact and communicate with others and how we form relationships

iii) Diseases which are carried in the blood, semen and other body fluids, or in the genitals, which are transmitted through sexual intercourse

iv) Having a close relationship with something

v) The way you think about yourself, the way the world sees you and the characteristics that define you

vi) The characteristics that someone or something has

vii) A group of people who share a particular set of beliefs

viii) A part we play in relation to others

ix) The ability to keep trying, no matter how many failures you might have

x) A set of stories about things, such as how and why we were created and what happens after death

12 Read 9.8 in the Student's Book. Use the words in the box to complete the statements.

aware	community	friends	moral
nurture	responsibility	social	spiritually

Being part of a faith community will help us to:

a) _____ and satisfy children's needs

b) be _____ that there is a wider world

c) meet new _____ and help other people

d) become _____ aware

e) deal with _____ issues

f) help shape people's _____ character and help to develop a sense of _____

g) build a _____ of friends and a network of support